MW00892284

FLUMINENSE
BUTTERFLY

AMAZING ANIMALS

A Collection of Creatures

GREAT AND SMALL

HONEY POSSUM

STERLING CHILDREN'S BOOKS
New York

An Imprint of Sterling Publishing
1166 Avenue of the Americas
New York, NY 10036

Written by Camilla de la Bedoyere

First Sterling edition published in 2015.
Published by Sterling Publishing Co., Inc.

Originally published in 2013 in the United Kingdom by
QED Publishing
A Quarto Group Company
The Old Brewery
6 Blundell Street
London, N7 9BH

© 2013 by Marshall Editions

All rights reserved. No part of this publication may be reproduced, stored in a retrieval system, or transmitted in any form or by any means (including electronic, mechanical, photocopying, recording, or otherwise) without prior written permission from the publisher.

ISBN 978-14549-1458-7

Distributed in Canada by Sterling Publishing
c/o Canadian Manda Group, 664 Annette Street
Toronto, Ontario, Canada M6S 2C8

Manufactured in China
Lot #:
2 4 6 8 10 9 7 5 3 1
12/14

www.sterlingpublishing.com/kids

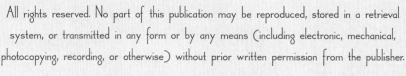

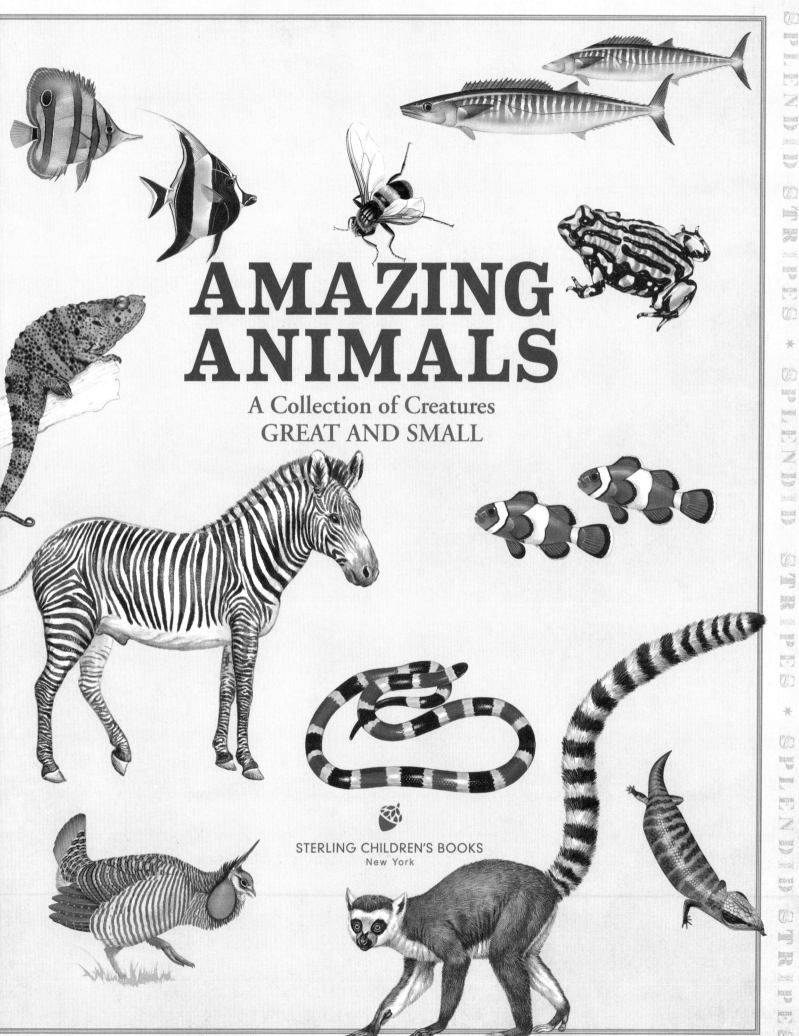

AMAZING ANIMALS

A Collection of Creatures
GREAT AND SMALL

STERLING CHILDREN'S BOOKS
New York

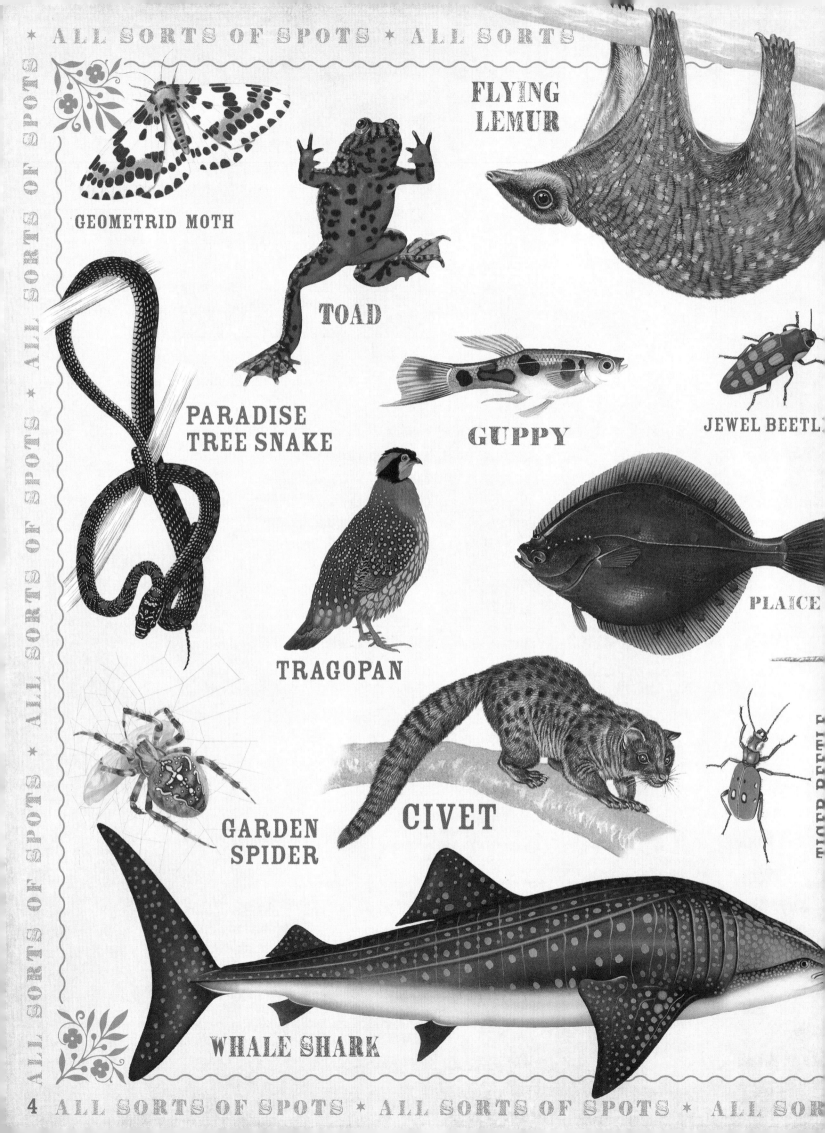

GEOMETRID MOTH

FLYING LEMUR

TOAD

PARADISE TREE SNAKE

GUPPY

JEWEL BEETLE

TRAGOPAN

PLAICE

GARDEN SPIDER

CIVET

TIGER BEETLE

WHALE SHARK

WHALEFISH

PEACOCK

LADYBUG

ANACONDA

TURTLE

NARWHAL

SALAMANDER

LEOPARD

DOLPHINFISH

RED SALAMANDER

RED HOWLER MONKEY

FALSE CORAL SNAKE

Red

RED FOX

CARDINAL

VELVET MITE

SCARLET TANAGER

ROUGHY

SIAMESE FIGHTING FISH

SHIELD BUG

RED KANGAROO

SHRIMP

CABBAGE WHITE BUTTERFLY
CATERPILLAR

CHAMELEON

LEOPARD FROG

LADYBUG

BLUE-CROWNED MOTMOT

PRAYING
MANTIS

BUTTERFLY

LEAF INSECT

Green

TIGER
SALAMANDER

SICKLEBILL

COPPER
BUTTERFLY
CATERPILLAR

GREEN
MAMBA SNAKE

SPIDER

GREEN ANOLE LIZARD

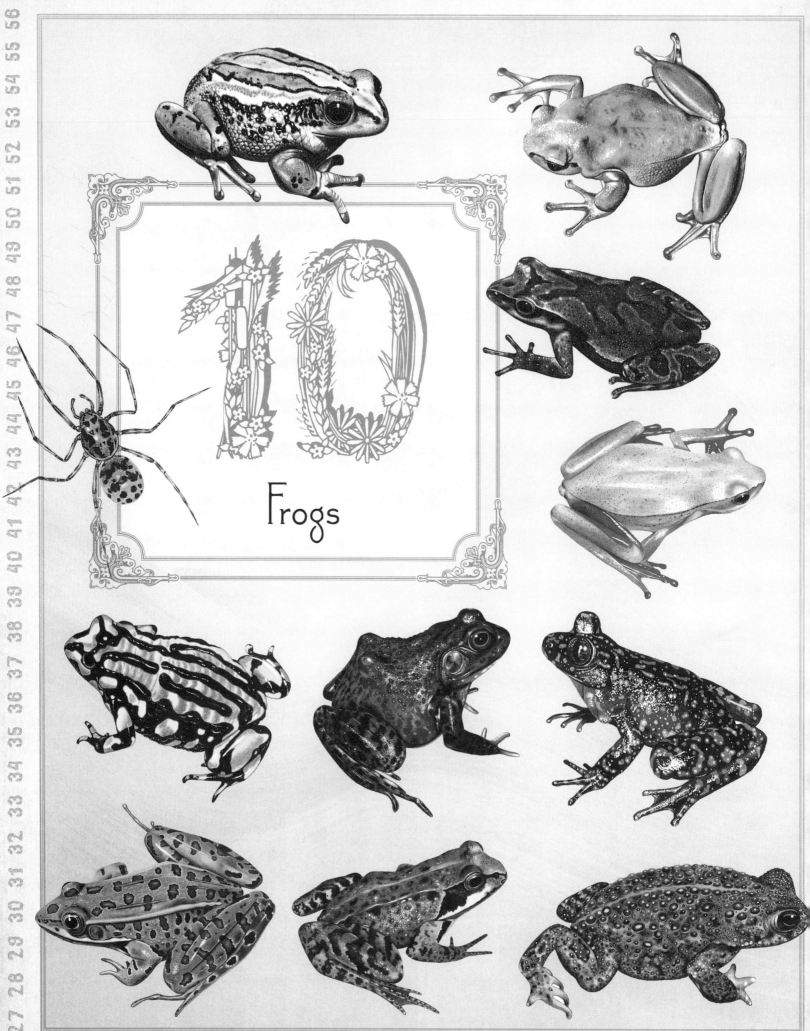

10

Frogs

20

Spiders

SPECTACLED CAIMAN

ROUGH-HEAD GRENADIER

HAMMERHEAD SHARK

BLOW FLY

WOLF SPIDER

BEE

SNOWY OWL

TURBOT

LOCUST

Most animals have two eyes. Which of these creatures has more than two?

ANSWER ON PAGE 64

WEB-FOOTED GECKO

SQUID

BEE

NAUTILUS

AYE-AYE

LAMP SHELL

ORNATE BOX
TURTLE

SWALLOWTAIL
BUTTERFLY

Yellow

YELLOWHAMMER

PLANT BUG

GOLDEN
ORIOLE

YELLOWTAIL
SNAPPER

ARUM
LILY FROG

YELLOW-THROATED
LONGCLAW

CRAB SPIDER

THORNY STARFISH

GREATER
FRUIT BAT

CLOWN
ANEMONEFISH

GOLDEN
POISON-ARROW
FROG

CARDINAL
CLICK BEETLE

Orange

METALMARK
BUTTERFLY

ORANGUTAN

GOLDFISH

ATLAS MOTH

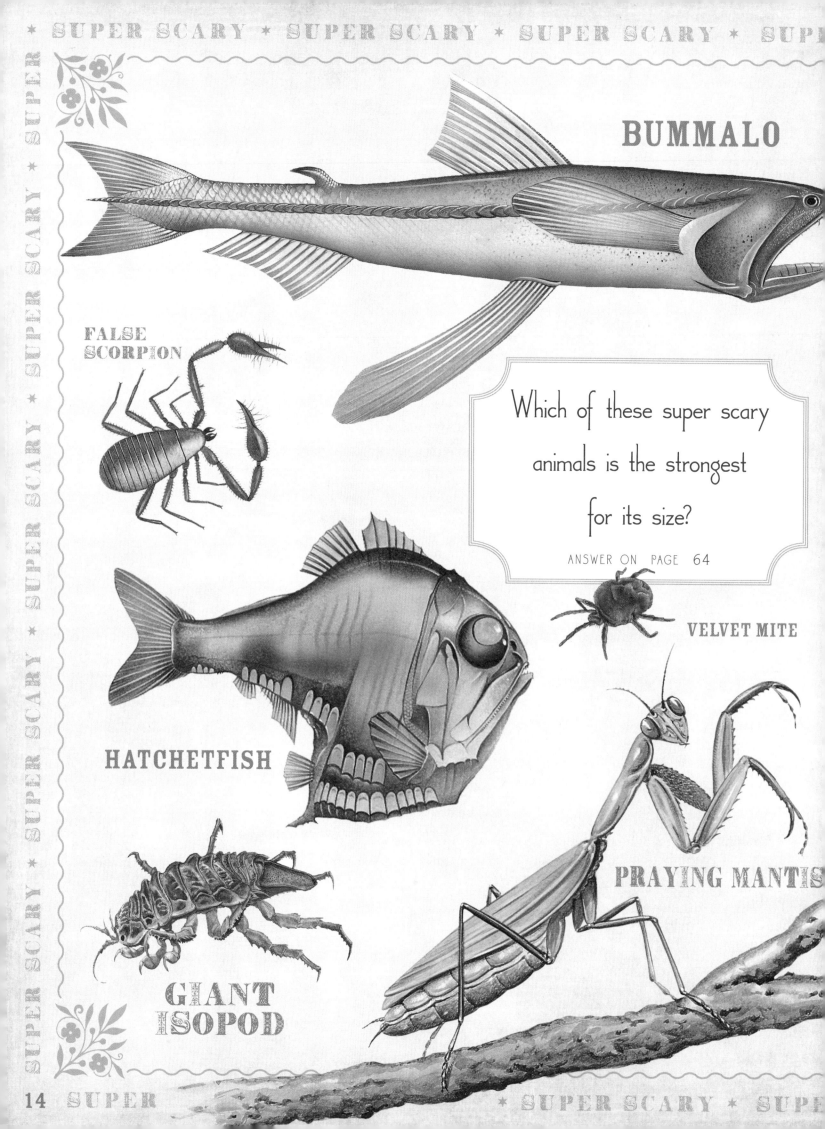

BUMMALO

FALSE SCORPION

Which of these super scary animals is the strongest for its size?

ANSWER ON PAGE 64

VELVET MITE

HATCHETFISH

PRAYING MANTIS

GIANT ISOPOD

SUPER SCARY ★ SUPER SCARY ★ SUPER

FLEA

LIONFISH

STAG BEETLE GRUB

TICK

DUST MITE

BOLL WEEVIL

STAG BEETLE

ANGLERFISH

PURSE WEB SPIDER

30
Ladybugs

40
Tadpoles

50
Butterflies and Moths

FENNEC FOX

KOALA

DEER MOUSE

GREAT JERBOA

LONG-EARED OWL

Find the animal with the smallest ears. It probably has the best hearing of the group. Which one is it?

ANSWER ON PAGE 64

LUNA MOTH

ELEPHANT SHREW

RABBIT

SPRINGHARE

GHOST
BAT

RACCOON

AFRICAN
HUNTING
DOG

LAPPET-FACED
VULTURE

AARDVARK

CHEETAH

SLUG

GIBBON

JUNGLE
RUNNER

MIDGE

GARDEN
SNAIL

HOUSEFLY

WEDDELL
SEAL

WOOD TURTLE

BOTTLENOSE
DOLPHIN

CATERPILLAR

GRASSHOPPER

RED-KNEED TARANTULA

THREE-TOED SLOTH

ROADRUNNER

HEDGEHOG

PIRANHA

FLEA

GREATER RHEA

If these animals had a race, which do you think would win?

ANSWER ON PAGE 64

EARWIG

ELEPHANT

RED DEER

STAG
BEETLE

PORCUPINE

MARLIN

BRITTLE
STAR

RHINOCEROS

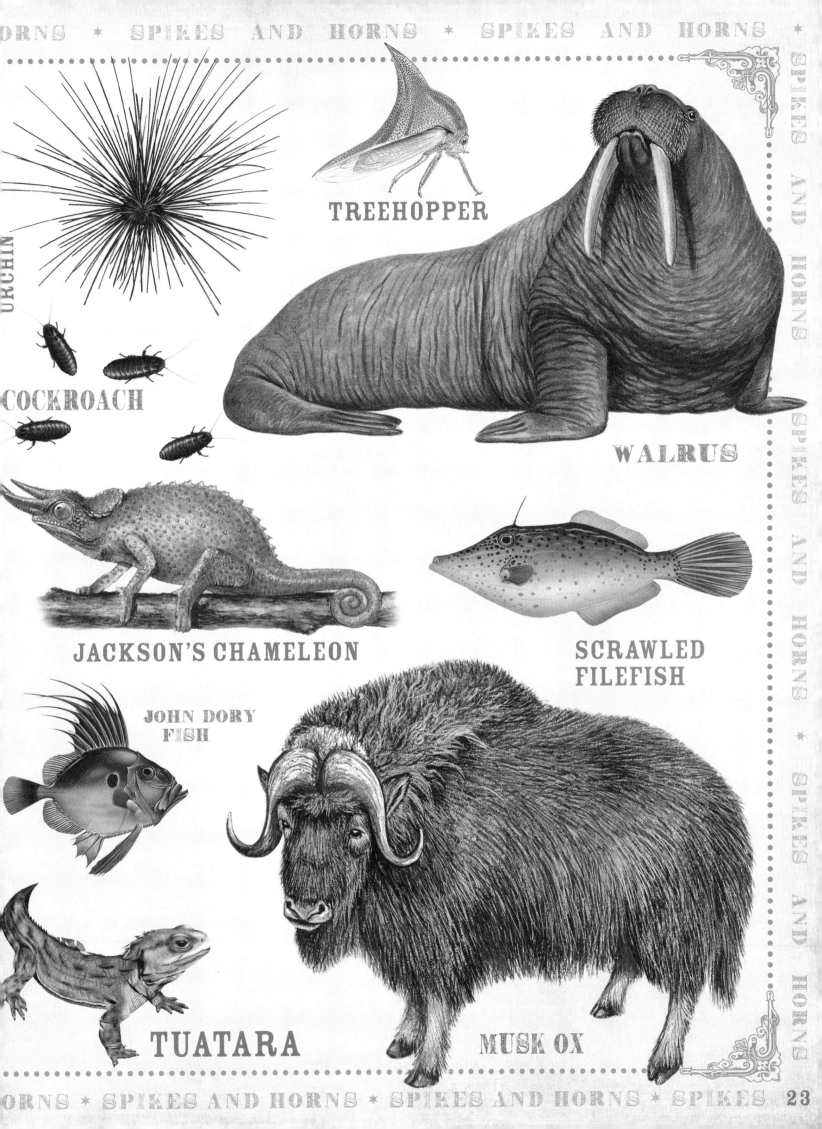

URCHIN

TREEHOPPER

COCKROACH

WALRUS

JACKSON'S CHAMELEON

SCRAWLED
FILEFISH

JOHN DORY
FISH

TUATARA

MUSK OX

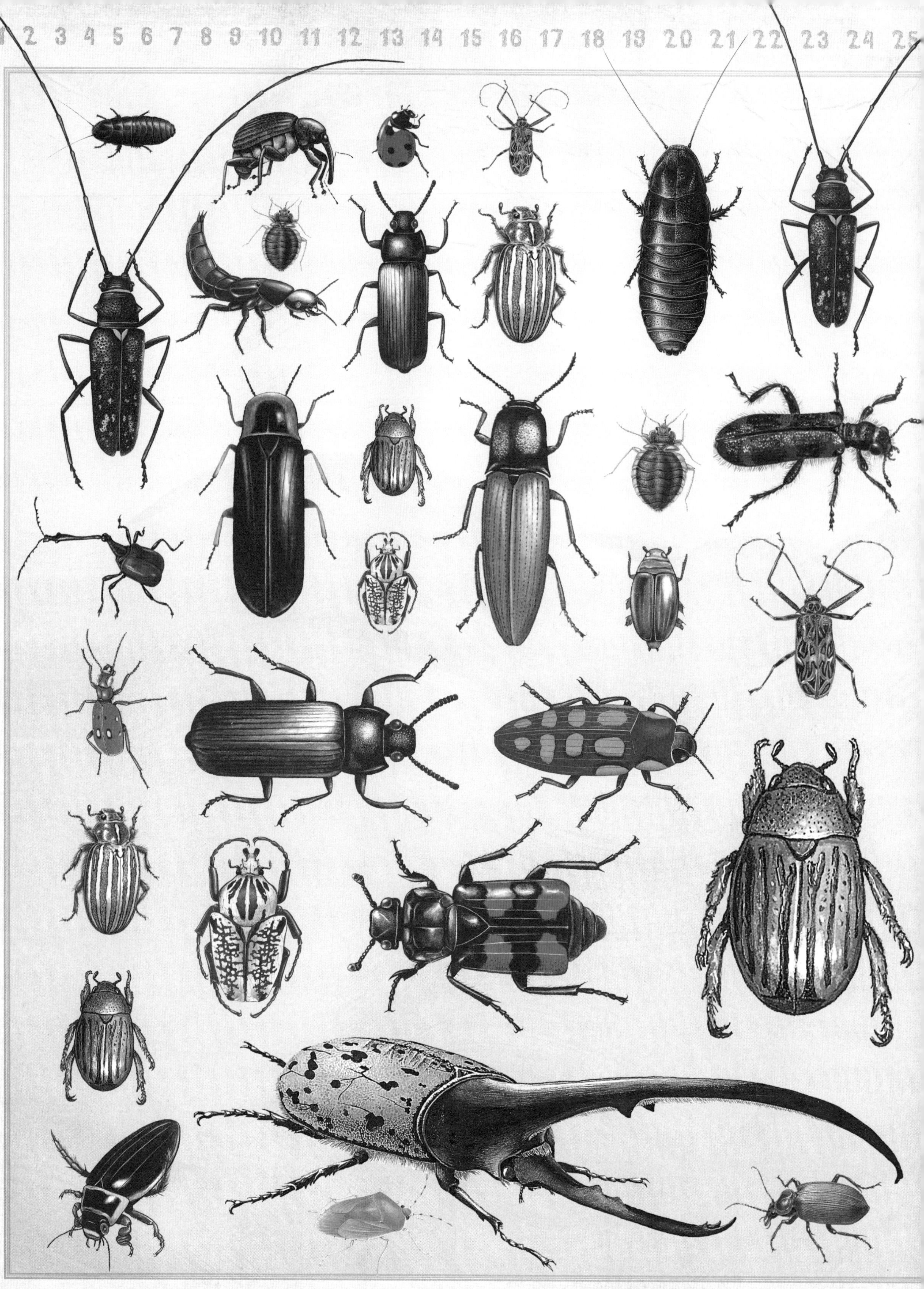

60

Beetles and Bugs

BLUE BIRD
OF PARADISE

RUBY-THROATED
HUMMINGBIRD

RED-TUFTED
MALACHITE
SUNBIRD

KING OF
SAXONY
BIRD

SUPERB
LYREBIRD

CRIMSON
TOPAZ

RAGGIANAS

MARVELOUS
SPATULETAIL

GREATER BIRD
OF PARADISE

QUETZAL

ROYAL
FLYCATCHER

WIRE-TAILED
MANAKIN

JEWEL BEETLE

BLOW FLY

SATIN
BOWERBIRD

BLUEFIN TUNA

Blue

DRAGONFLY

MORPHO
BUTTERFLY

SPOTTED SALAMANDER

LOBSTER

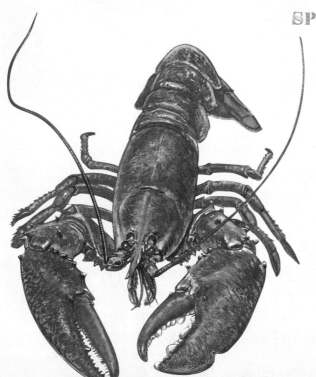

BLUE
JAY

JELLYFISH

PURPLE
HONEYCREEPER

Purple

PORTUGESE
MAN OF WAR

PUFFERFISH

AXOLOTL

CAECILIAN

FLOWER
MANTIS

KIWI

EIDER
DUCK

TOUCAN

FLAMINGO

RAINBOW
LORIKEET

TURKEY

PUFFIN

SPARROW

AVOCET

ROOSTER

GOSHAWK

HUMMINGBIRD

BROWN PELICAN

HORNBILL

OYSTERCATCHER

70

Lizards and Salamanders

CATERPILLAR

ANT

WREN

OSTRICH

SHRIMP

GIRAFFE

MINNOWS

BEDBUG

ELEPHANT

HUMMINGBIRD

HIPPOPOTAMUS

MOUSE

SILVERFISH

SPERM WHALE

GOLDEN LION
TAMARIN

PANAMANIAN
GOLD FROG

DESERT
KANGAROO RAT

SILVERFISH

Gold

FALSE
SCORPION

GOLDEN
MOUSE

IMPALA

LIONS

HAMSTER

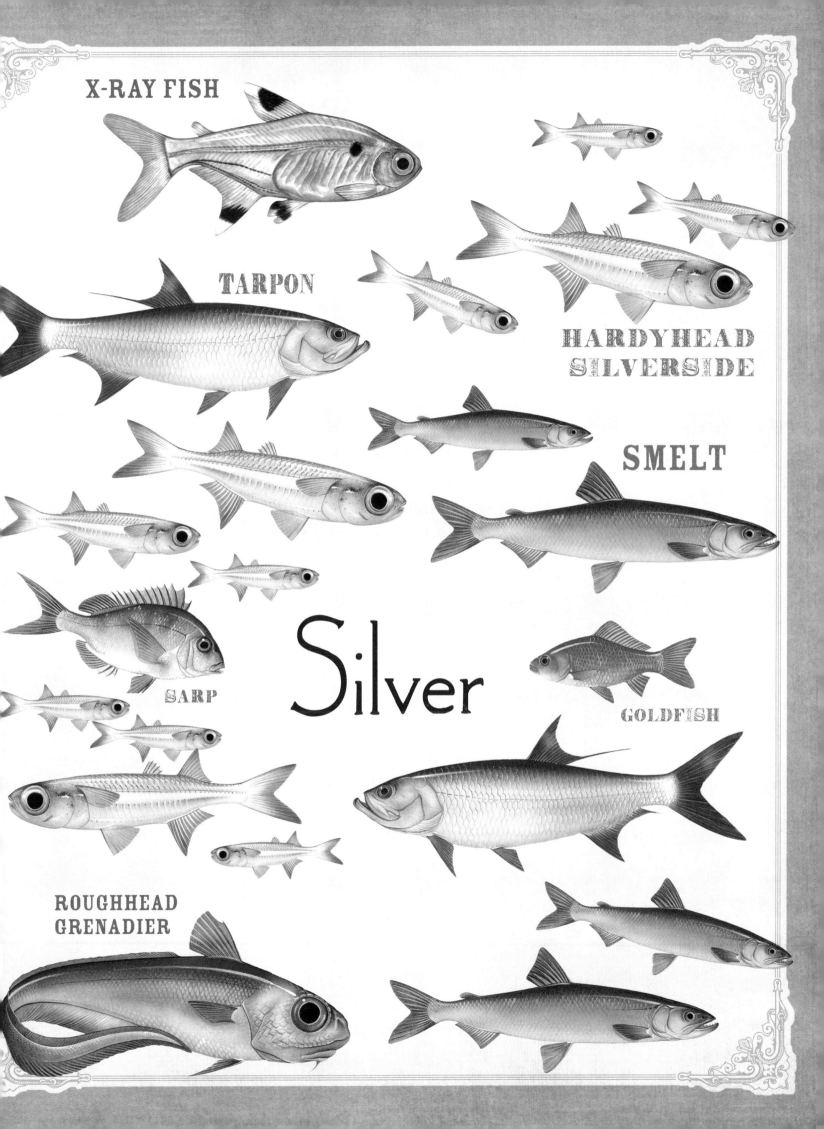

X-RAY FISH

TARPON

HARDYHEAD
SILVERSIDE

SMELT

Silver

SARP

GOLDFISH

ROUGHHEAD
GRENADIER

WILD BOAR

ELEPHANT
SHREW

INDIAN
ELEPHANT

PADDLEFISH

LOWLAND
STREAKED
TENREC

MANATEE

ECHIDNA

PROBOSCIS MONKEY

GAVIAL CROCODILE

TAPIR

What can use its nose to carry water, pick things up, and stroke its baby?

ANSWER ON PAGE 64

GANGES DOLPHIN

GIANT ANTEATER

DARWIN'S FROG

80

Penguins

BLUE-BLACK
SPIDER WASP

AFRICAN PENGUIN

NORTHERN
JACANA

HARP
SEAL

STICK INSECT

Do animals with many legs move faster than those with just two?

ANSWER ON PAGE 64

GALAPAGOS GIANT
TORTOISE

FUNNEL-WEB
SPIDER

GREAT JERBOA

CRANE FLY

WALLACE'S FLYING FROG

MILLIPEDE

SEA LION

CENTIPEDE

GREEN TURTLE

ANT

GERBIL

LONGHORN BEETLE

BEAVER

BLACK WIDOW
SPIDER

GREATER SIREN
SALAMANDER

PANDA

ROVE
BEETLE

Black

ATLANTIC MANTA

GOLIATH BEETLE

GORILLA

POLAR BEAR

ARABIAN ORYX

ARCTIC HARE

WHITE WHALE

MUTE SWAN

White

GREAT EGRET

CLAM

ARCTIC FOX

GREAT BLACK SLUG

90

Flying insects

SAILFISH

VELVET ANT

OLEANDER
SPHINX MOTH

FOOTBALL
FISH

SEA LILY

SOUTH AFRICAN
RAIN FROG

CHAMELEON

SEA
ANEMONE

MOLE CRICKET

INDRI

ROBBER FLY

GLASS FROG

Which of these animals carries its babies in an unusual way?

ANSWER ON PAGE 64

OCEAN SUNFISH

HERMIT IBIS

CROCODILE

CORROBOREE FROG

SUN
BITTERN

GREATER GLIDER

EARWIG

COMMON

BROWN LONG-EARED BAT

MIDGE

WARBLE

OSTRICH

FLYING
FISH

STORM
PETREL

HUMMINGBIRD MOTH

GREAT
BLACK-BACKED
GULL

QUEEN ALEXANDRA'S
BIRDWING

What appears to fly but
doesn't have wings?

ANSWER ON PAGE 64

ANTLION

RED KITE

STINGRAY

KING VULTURE

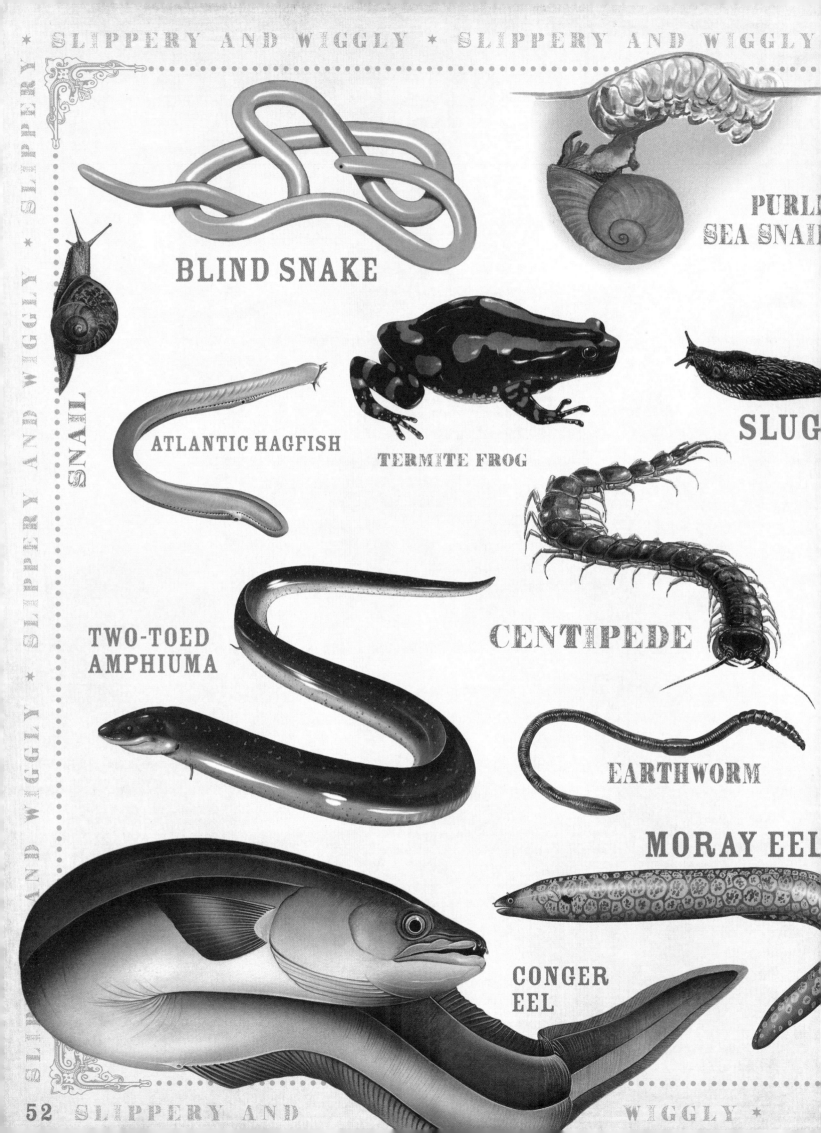

BLIND SNAKE

PURPLE
SEA SNAIL

SNAIL

ATLANTIC HAGFISH

TERMITE FROG

SLUG

TWO-TOED
AMPHIUMA

CENTIPEDE

EARTHWORM

MORAY EEL

CONGER
EEL

TRANSVAAL
SNAKE
LIZARD

OCTOPUS

NUDIBRANCH

SPOTTED
WATER SNAKE

LAMPREY

CAECILIAN

PACIFIC GIANT
SALAMANDER

ROSS
SEAL

PADDLE WORM

100

Fish

RED-TAILED
TROPIC BIRD

EMPEROR
TAMARIN

OLM

CAPE LOPEZ
LYRETAIL

GUPPY

KOWARI

Which of these creatures

has a stinger?

ANSWER ON PAGE 64

SCORPION

ZORILLA

WEEDY
SEADRAGON

MELLER'S
CHAMELEON

CLUBTAIL
DRAGONFLY

MAYFLY

LUMHOLTZ'S TREE
KANGAROO

RED
SQUIRREL

MACAW

DESERT
KANGAROO RAT

TREE
PANGOLIN

STONEFIS

LUMPSUCKER

STURGEON

ARABIAN
TOAD-HEADED
AGAMA

GIANT
TOAD

PINECONE
FISH

GIANT ARMADILLO

FIDDLER CRAB

WARTY
NEWT

SAND DOLLAR

ALLIGATOR
SNAPPING TURTLE

ARMADILLO LIZARD

DWARF SEAHORSE

SEA
CUCUMBER

SALTWATER
CROCODILE

GHOST BAT

GOOSE
BARNACLE

SCALLOP

FUNNEL-WEB
SPIDER

Only mammals have real hair.
Which animals are faking it?

ANSWER ON PAGE 64

FIREBRAT

SURUBIM

AARDWOLF

MANED
WOLF

PORCUPINE
FISH

WHITE-LINED
SPHINX MOTH

ARMY
ANT

JAPANESE MACAQUE

CARPENTER BEE

SUMATRAN
RHINO

SUN BEAR

SEA MOUSE

WIND SCORPION

ARCTIC
HARE

PENGUINS

CRABEATER SEAL

NORWAY
LEMMING

POLAR
BEAR

MOOSE

GERBOA

SECRETARY
BIRD

GREEN
IGUANA

INDIAN
PYTHON

FIREFLY

DESERT NIGHT
LIZARD

CAMEL

INTERESTING EYES

Most animals have two eyes. This wolf spider has eight.

WOLF SPIDER

STAG BEETLE

SUPER SCARY

The stag beetle is incredibly strong for its size, making it one of the world's strongest beasts.

LUNA MOTH

SLUG

SNAI

WEIRD EARS

The moth has very simple ears and can hear better than almost any other animal!

FAST AND SLOW

The cheetah would win. It can reach a top speed of more than 60 miles per hour.

INDIAN ELEPHANT

CENTIPEDE

NIFTY NOSES

The elephant's nose is called a trunk; it is really strong and very useful.

LEGS AND FEET

Four legs are faster than two, but for its size, the spider, ant, and centipede can move very fast with more!

SPIDER

ANT

GREATER GLIDER

SCORPION

CROCODILE

TREMENDOUS TAILS

The scorpion protects itself from predators by using its tail to sting.

FABULOUS WINGS

The glider's skin and the fish's pectoral fins help them glide, but neither have wings to fly.

WEIRD AND WONDERFUL

The crocodile carries its young in an unusual way. It holds them in its mouth!

FLYING FISH

GHOST BAT

INCREDIBLY HAIRY

These are the mammals with real hair. The rest are faking it.

AARDWOLF

MANED WOLF

JAPANESE MACAQUE

SUN BEAR

SUMATRAN RH